The Casanova
Killer

The Shocking True
Story of Serial Killer
Paul John Knowles

Roger Harrington

Table of Contents

Introduction

Paul John Knowles, known as the Casanova Killer was the exact opposite of his legendary romantic namesake. One of the most unique killers of the twentieth century, Knowles terrorized the United States in a cross country murder spree from July to November 1974. Instead of wooing women, romancing them and leaving like his namesake the real-life Casanova, Knowles adding another step in the process; murder.

There were some similarities between Paul Knowles and his namesake. Knowles was described as a "dreamboat" by a would-be victim and romantic partner. Although once she saw his true self behind the handsome face, she quickly changed her tune.

Knowles was not the model of a classic serial killer who possessed outward normality and the facade of respectability. Instead, he was a ruthless, vicious rampage and spree killer with no regard for human life and no clear M.O.

The victims of the Casanova Killer's spree were not just women. Knowles murdered men, women, and children of all ages. His inconsistent victim profile and M.O would have made his capture almost impossible. Also, the fact that the murders he committed over four months were committed in different states also made him impossible to apprehend.

His constant traveling as well as the time period in which his killings took place before technology became as prevalent as it today led to Knowles not even being on the police's radar as a suspect for some time. At this time, law enforcement communication was also not as common as it is today.

Not as much is known about the man know referred to as the Casanova Killer as the majority of his crimes took place in a short amount of time. Knowles's own untimely death at the hands of law enforcement shortly after his apprehension is one of the many reasons why we know so little about the handsome man who terrorized over half the country for four months.

Knowles murdered so many people during his short active killing period that the numbers equated to around one victim per week for the rest of his life.

His dramatic and abrupt end left many unanswered questions about his life, psychological makeup, and his motives for killing. Had Knowles lived longer and sadly

The Casanova Killer's spree took the lives of at least 18 people. Unlike most infamous killing sprees, this one left two women who were lucky enough to get away and be spared their life. One of these women was a reporter by then the name of Sandy Fawkes whose account of Knowles has become the definitive source for all things Paul John Knowles.

Knowles also left behind a series of confession tapes which he recorded during his travels. Unfortunately, the tapes were kept in the courthouse in Macon, Georgia after Knowles was apprehended and were later destroyed in a flood. Everything that is known about his murders is secondhand making the details even more murky and complicated.

While law enforcement and the families of known victims were presumably able to get some closure from Knowles's death, the real questions behind why his killing spree began and an insight into the killers own is missing from the narrative. — all theories

These holes in the story have been filled in over the years in order for investigators to finish the manuscript and fully understand Knowles's motives and psychology. Just because there are many unanswered questions about the Casanova Killer doesn't mean the story of his four-month killing spree isn't worth telling.

most part of chapter forming sympathy to Knowles before telling his story

Early Life and Crimes

Paul John Knowles was born in Orlando, Florida on April 25, 1946 to Thomas and Bonnie Knowles. Other sources have noted other various dates in April for his birthday. Not much is known about his childhood or his parents. *— contradicting*

Knowles's own father gave up custody of him when he was a young child as Mr. Knowles had been arrested for various crimes, a fate his son would soon follow. *assumption stereotype.*

Knowles was raised his various foster homes until he became a legal adult. This unstable upbringing and lack of a normal, stable family environment is a common trait among serial and spree killers. His first brush with crime occurred when he was only seven years old when he stole a bicycle.

Knowles also refused to do homework and listen to teachers. Even though Knowles performed poorly in school, he was highly intelligent and was an avid reader. During one of his prison sentences, he scored extremely high on an intelligence test is given to the inmates.

During his childhood, he also showed little respect to other authority figures including his parents. This early lack of respect for authority and the law was a clear sign of bigger things to come in the future. As Knowles grew older, he found that he enjoyed the attention he received from his peers by acting out and distracting adults. His behavior made Knowles popular among his peers but for negative reasons.

7

Knowles was known to misbehave in school and then report what he'd done to his friends who would then laugh and praise him for his behavior. This led to Knowles seeking attention, something that would continue throughout his adult life.

trustworthy sorce?

When Knowles was a young child, he told a friend that when he grew up that he "wanted to be a big, famous bad guy," which is exactly what he did. Friends also said that Knowles loved reading about famous criminals and outlaws.

He was especially big fans of both Bonnie and Clyde as well as John Dillinger, which is ironic considering these criminals all traveled across the country committing their crimes and met dramatic ends in shootouts with the police just like Knowles would.

Those who knew him said that Knowles always had a bad temper even as a child. Some stated that his violent tendencies manifested early. Knowles reportedly showed aggression towards his female classmates and relatives from any early age. —examples?

A sister of a friend of Knowles said that he loved the aforementioned attention he received from his violent behavior and that if he didn't get it. The sister of one of Knowles once said that he punched a girl in the face for rejecting his advances. Knowles figured out from an early age that committing crimes and getting in trouble would get him the attention he so craved.

This desire and drive for constant attention is also believed to have led to Knowles many romantic relationships throughout his relatively short life. The constant female attention served as a boost to his ego. The romantic and sexual relationships he garnered with these women, many of who would become his victims, was also a way for Knowles to exert control over another person.

His early lack of respect for authority and the fact that he didn't do his homework was a part of his issues with control including having control over another person. In Knowles mind, not completing his homework was a way for him to exert control over the authority figures in his life. These issues with control later spilled into his murders as a part of serial killing is establishing control over another person by having the power of ending their life.

When Knowles was a teenager, he was sent to the Florida School for Boys in Marianna,

10

Florida. Knowles sent to the reform school and juvenile detention center for several criminal charges including breaking and entering and grand larceny.

The Florida School for Boys had a notorious reputation that dated back through the then-111 year history. Guards, teachers, and other employees of the detention center were known to abuse, torture, and even murder the juveniles in their custody. At this time in the United States, reform schools which were similar to modern-day juvenile detention facilities, focused on behavior modification for juvenile offenders instead of punishment.

When the school closed and was demolished in 2011, construction workers found the remains of over 50 students who had been murdered there. Some believe that there were even more victims that were covered up from the media and police to protect any former employees who might still be alive as well as the state government.

In 1968, during the last year of Knowles reform school sentence, the Florida governor paid a visit to the school. There he saw the students living in horrible conditions and being abused. After his visit of the facility, all corporal punishment was banned in Florida reform schools.

Knowles time in the reform school as a young child is believed to have had significant damage to his mental state. The abuse and repeated corporal punishment Knowles experienced was a leading cause to his later deranged mental state.

/ vague

A study on the childhood of serial killers showed that 42% were abused either physically or mentally during their childhoods and Paul John Knowles was no different. This abuse and the degradation it caused as well as the lack of control these killers experienced while being abused manifests within them as children and later comes out during their killings.

Knowles's second arrest occurred when he was twenty-three, and for a crime that was much more advanced than a previous juvenile offender. One night in March 1969, Knowles, now "aged out" of foster care and reform schools, stole a car.

Once the police chased him down in the stolen car, Knowles pulled over. When the officer approached Knowles in the stolen vehicle, Knowles was able to get out of the car, steal the police officer's gun and take him hostage. Knowles freed the officer after a non-violent two-hour standoff with police.

This indecent in 1969 was not the first time Knowles had kidnapped a police officer. Four years prior, at age 19, Knowles had committed the same crime after he pulled a sawed-off shotgun on a police officer when he was pulled over.

These two incidents of kidnapping a police officer were only the beginning for the long list of crimes that the future held for Paul John Knowles, nor would it be the last time he attempted to kidnap a police officer. These incidents of kidnapping police officers are a nod to his issues with respecting authority figures.

By kidnapping authority figures who are in constant control, Knowles was shifting the

/theory

power dynamics between civilian and authority figure. He was finally in charge and was able to assert his dominance over someone more powerful than him. In turn, this gave Knowles the feeling of superiority he wanted.

Knowles was sentenced to several years in prison for the kidnapping of the police officer as well as grand theft auto and burglary. Knowles was sentenced to serve time at Raiford Prison which is now known as the Florida State Prison.

Raiford Prison is also known for housing two other famous American serial killers; Ted Bundy, Ottis Toole, and Aileen Wuornos.

Bundy and Wuronos were both executed in the prison in 1989 and in 2002. Ottis Toole, the famed accomplice and serial killer to fellow killer Henry Lee Lucas died in Raiford Prison in 1996.

Raiford Prison is also famous for being the subject of a song by the rock band Lynyrd Skynyrd called "Four Walls of Raiford."

The prison is also one of the only prisons left in the United States that will still allow inmates sentenced to death to choose either the electric chair or lethal injection.

His time in Raiford was the first of many prison and jail sentences for Knowles. From 1969 until his death in 1974, Knowles had the distinction of spending up to six months out of every year therein behind bars.

While he was incarcerated, Knowles began corresponding with several women. His relationships with women were plentiful and seemingly successful for some time.

The image of Knowles and the reputation he received in the media which still persist to this day, is that he was a suave womanizer.

In a sense, he was but based on the facts and evidence related to the murders he committed, Knowles used his good looks and superficial, sociopathic charm as a weapon to lure both men and women to him in order to eventually kill them.

After he was apprehended, the media used his romantic relationships and his strikingly handsome good looks to catalpas and sensationalize the Casanova Killer nickname and image. └─> calling out media-makes him seem trustworthy

One was a woman named Jackie Knight. Knowles and Knight met in person at a bar during one of the rare times he was not in prison. His relationship with Jackie Knight was not ideal for him as she was married.

That night at the bar. Knowles also met Jackie's husband. The three all got along very well and the Knights soon introduced Knowles to their three children. On one occasion, Knowles who said to have liked the Knight children even accompanied the family to an outing at a local county fair.

Knowles soon went back to prison. Jackie Knight continued writing to him as well as got divorced. The two grew closer and their relationship finally became romantic. Knowles soon proposed to her via a letter. Jackie accepted his proposal.

On May 10, 1970, Knowles was released from Raiford Prison. He and Jackie were married shortly after his release. Knowles finally had security and a family, something that he wouldn't have for very long.

After their wedding, Knowles sought gainful employment but could not find a decent job due to his extensive criminal history and lack of career experience. To help make ends meet, Knowles begin meeting up with his group of friends who were also known criminals.

This meeting with his old group of friends echoed his childhood experiences of acting out and misbehaving to gain the attention and approval of his friends. It is unknown what led to Knowles and Jackie to break-up. However, it is believed that his association with his known criminal friends was a major factor.

In 1971, only a year after their wedding, Jackie moved several hours away from their home in Orlando, Florida with her three children to

Macon, Georgia. There she had their marriage annulled. Despite their failed marriage and annulment, the two remained friends. Knowles would often visit Jackie and her children during the rare times he was not incarcerated.

In 1972, Knowles was arrested yet again for burglary. Later that year he was released into a prison furlough program. This is a program where inmates are released into their communities for short periods of time either for personal reasons, to find work once they are released on parole, or to slowly integrate them back into society.

While Knowles was on this program, he was out one day and failed to return back to prison. This resulted in another criminal charge for escape and earned him an additional three years to his sentence.

Once back in prison, Knowles started corresponding with a woman in San Francisco, California named Angela Covic, a young divorcee who was working as a cocktail waitress. Knowles found Angela Covic after reading an article about her American Astrology Magazine as her mother was a well-known psychic.

Knowles was a big believer in astrology and followed his daily horoscope readings religiously. Those who knew Knowles reported that his daily horoscope had a great effect on his mood. On days where his readings did not say what he wanted them to, or if the predictions were negative Knowles was known to be in a very bad mood and often let his infamous temper show on these days.

During the years after his brief marriage to Jackie Knight fell apart, Knowles was in and out of jail more than ever before. He described himself during this time as being "angry and aimless." These sour moods and hopelessness Knowles was feeling at this time would have been a reason why he was so interested in and followed his horoscopes.

After corresponding back and forth with Angela Covic, Knowles moods changed. The two fell in love after only sending a few letters to one another. Covic soon traveled to Florida to meet Knowles. Impressed by his good looks, as many women were, the two began a romantic relationship after corresponding with him as pen pals for several months.

The couple became engaged in 1974 after Knowles proposed to Covic during her prison visit. Knowles and Covic had only exchanged a few letters before their meeting and After their engagement, Covic worked tirelessly for Knowles's release by paying for his legal counsel. All of her hard work and legal fees paid off and Knowles was granted parole in 1974.

Covic was not deterred by his criminal past and record as her first husband also had a criminal past. Covic even gave him the nickname "Mad Dog Knowles." Knowles started calling her "my Yiddish angel."

His relationship with Covic inspired Knowles to want to change his life for the better. While still in prison and corresponding with Covic he obtained his high school diploma in hopes of obtaining legitimate employment after his release. Once be obtained his high school diploma, Knowles also started taking college courses in prison. Knowles hoped to obtain a job as a sign painter when he was released.

There has been some debate over the relationship between Knowles and Covic with some estimating that his intentions with her were not based on romantic feelings, instead, he was using her as a way out of prison.

This has never been proven and is only speculation. However, the fact that Knowles was going to move away from his old life and friends who got him into trouble for Covic potentially proves otherwise.

Knowles also stated that this time with Covic he wanted to change his life for the better and finally give up on his life of crime.

Covic hired a Miami, Florida lawyer named Sheldon Yavitz to defend him. Yavitz was well-known inches home state as the lawyer who defended South Florida's many murderers, gangsters, and drug dealers. He was known for getting many of his clients off on various technicalities. His unsavory client base made him the perfect fit to defend Knowles.

Yavitz was able to get Knowles an early prison release. Knowles moved to California with Covic after his release on May 14, 1974.

Their brief relationship soon crumbled when Covic was introduced to Knowles's true ways. The couple only lived together for a week. She later recalled that he "projected an aura of fear."

Sensing trouble, Covic broke up their relationship after her mother (and her better judgment) told her not to marry him and warned her of a dangerous new man in her life.

Covic kicked Knowles out of her house, ended their relationship, and called off their wedding. The break-up both devastated Knowles and set off his murderous rampage that would take the lives of up to 35 people and span several months and several states.

The Cross Country Killing Casanova

The night Angela Covic broke off their relationship Knowles later claimed to have murdered three people in the streets of San Francisco. Their breakup was no doubt a major blow to Knowles self-esteem and completely derailed his life plan to get on the straight and narrow for the first time ever. The blow was too much to take and the rejection set Knowles off on a rampage as well as threw him back in the life he so wanted to leave.

These three murderers were never confirmed by authorities but Knowles continued to claim the three San Francis murders even after he was apprehended. If he really did commit the three murders, then his fourth in a long time of murders happened soon after.

Since the San Francis murders are not officially included in Knowles count, his first official murder was that of Alice Curtis, a 65-year-old school teacher in Jacksonville, Florida.

After Angela Covic broke up with Knowles, he returned back to his home state. Instead of going back to his hometown and his criminal friends who continually had been getting him in trouble for years, Knowles briefly settled in Jacksonville, a city several hours away from his hometown of Orlando.

On the night of July 26, 1974, Knowles went on an alcohol bender. He ended up picking a fight with a bouncer at a bar in Jacksonville. Knowles stabbed the bouncer and was arrested. Once in jail he picked the lock of the cell and stuck to his tried and true crime…escape.

Knowles was able to evade Jacksonville police and broke into the home of Alice Curtis. Curtis was found the next day bound and gagged. While it is believed Knowles did not set out to kill Curtis, the gag and restraints caused her to choke to death on her own dentures. It is unknown if Knowles was present when Curtis died.

It is believed that if Knowles did see Curtis die then he fled the scene to avoid a murder charge as he knew with his extensive criminal record which included violent crimes that there was no chance of a defense. Regardless of his intentions with Curtis, Knowles was responsible for her death whether it was an accident or not.

Knowles then ransacked her home, stole some valuables, and her 1971 yellow Dodge Demon.

Knowles later recalled that after he broke into Alice Curtis's home that the only choice he had was to run as he didn't want to go back to prison.

An associate of Knowles recalled that he said the only thing that actually scared Knowles was dying in prison by the electric chair. Knowles clearly made his choice to run and later recalled that he had gotten his chance to finally be a famous outlaw like the ones he'd admired growing up.

Knowles never told anyone whether or not he had intentionally killed Alice Curtis.

When authorities cleaned out his prison cell in Florida after he was released, they found a letter he'd written to Angela Covic where he compared himself to Bonnie and Clyde.

In the letter he wrote, "after this, I'm going to be famous."

Little did Knowles know, the death of Alice Curtis was the start of his four-month killing spree that would finally make him into the "big, famous bad guy" he'd always wanted to be.

In his old prison cell, authorities also found a photo of an electric chair that he'd cut out of a magazine. While it is unknown why he had this photo of his biggest fear, he most likely cut it out as a way to remind himself where he didn't want to end up.

The next victims during his murder spree met their fates only five days later still in Jacksonville, Florida.

Still driving around town in Alice Curtis's car, he soon realized he was a suspect in her death. Knowles was also known to have kept newspaper clippings about his murders as he was obsessed with the fame that being a famous outlaw would bring.

In the regards to his obsession with the fame that committing his crimes would bring, Knowles has been compared to Charles Manson.

Manson shared a similar philosophy when it came to his own crimes. Unlike Mason, Knowles had no political motivations in committing his crimes nor did he have a clear M.O.

Knowles killed his next victims on the night of August 1, 1974. That night a woman named Elizabeth Anderson left her two daughters,

Lillian and Mylette Anderson home alone to run an errand while her husband, Jack stayed late at work.

When Jack Addison returned home, Lillian and Mylette were missing. The Anderson's were immediately suspicions as it was unlike the girls to run off and leave the house. Both girls had health problems, Lillian had asthma and Mylette had thyroid problems and they knew to always have their medications with them.

The girls were not found for several months. Neighbors reported seeing a yellow car on their street the days Lillian and Mylette disappeared. At the time, no one had made a connection between the Anderson girls disappearance and the Alice Curtis murder.

The true fate of the Anderson sisters was not discovered until after Knowles was apprehended and killed. In his possessions, they found a tape recorder that Knowles had stolen from the home of a victim. The tapes included confessions Knowles had made about each of his victims.

Knowles confessed on the tape that he saw the Anderson sisters on the street where he was planning to dump Alice Curtis's car. If he hadn't seen the sisters, they would still be alive as Knowles was a family friend, his mother, Bonnie was friends with their mother, Elizabeth.

Blame?

Knowles had little to do with his family throughout his life, especially after his father sent him to a foster home as a child. There is also very little about his family in records available online.

Fearing that the young sisters would tell their parents they saw him with the yellow car and that their parents would tell the police, who then would connect him to the murder of Alice Curtis, they became his next victims.

Knowles kidnapped the sisters, strangled them, and put their bodies in a nearby swamp. Their bodies were never found.

Their father, Jack Anderson refused to believe his daughters had been murdered by Knowles as their bodies were never found. It wasn't until over a decade after Jack died that Elizabeth had tombstones and graves made for their daughters.

Knowles abandoned his plan to dump Alice Curtis's car and continued driving around in the car even though it was a huge risk to his potential capture.

Considering Knowles obsession with fame and being an outlaw, it makes sense that he would continue driving around in a piece of evidence connecting him to one of his murders.

This behavior is indicative to potentially wanting to get caught as this is a common trait among serial killers. Many serial killers including Knowles want the notoriety and attention from their crimes as many of them consider their crimes "their work" and want the world to know what they've done.

The desire to get caught is common in those killers who see themselves as doing the world a favor by eliminating a certain group or demographic. While Knowles had no M.O or victim profile, he most likely kept the car to add to the thrill of being an outlaw and for the thrill and rush that killing gave him.

generalisation

Knowles killed his next victim the following day on August 2, 1974. In Atlantic Beach, Florida, a small town east of Jacksonville, he met Majorie Howe, age 49.

The day Howe was murdered, her neighbor told police that a young man about six feet tall with light brown hair knocked on her door looking for a woman named Betty Johnson.

This was a tactic used by Knowles to get people to open their doors, catch them off guard, and let them inside. The neighbor told police that she wouldn't let him in her house. She also reported that the man had light brown hair even though Knowles had distinct red hair.

The neighbor saying the man had a different hair color could be attributed to Knowles' hair looking different in a certain light or the notoriously unreliability of eyewitness

↗Blame again?

testimonies. The neighbor did say something that was eventually used to link Knowles to Howe's murder.

She mentioned the distinct demon decal on the back of the yellow car the man was driving.

At the time, all Dodge Demons (the stolen car Knowles was driving that belonged to Alice Curtis) had a small red demon decal on the back. This detail is what led the police to connect Knowles to Howe's murder.

It is believed that Knowles tried the Betty Johnson tactic on Howe. Once inside her house, Knowles strangled her with one of her nylon stockings.

After killing Howe, Knowles stole a rifle and a television from her home. He ended up giving the television to his ex-wife, Jackie Knight.

While Knowles did not have an M.O like most killers, he tended to favor strangulation. He especially appeared to enjoy strangling women with their nylon stockings or pantyhose.

Strangulation is a common murder method with crimes of opportunity, as no other weapons are needed other than the killer's hands or an easily accessible item such as the victim's clothing. As the killings Knowles committed were random and unorganized (one of the main serial killer typologies) strangulation perfectly aligns with his unclear and opportunistic M.O.

Using an item of the victim's as intimate as underwear as a murder weapon is a hallmark trait of a lust killer.

Lust killers murder for sexual gratification and engage in rape, necrophilia, multination, and

Blame

39

sometimes blood drinking. In some of his later murders, Knowles admitted to having raped some of his victims as well as attempted necrophilia on another.

Rape and sexual violence during killings are connected to control and domination, something Knowles had issues with throughout his life. —Contradicting

Killers who also commit sexual murders usually have violent fantasies about rape and murder. Since engaging in those acts does little to satisfy and/or compare to the fantasies, that is why these deranged killers will continue committing the same crimes over and over again.

 Since the murders Knowles committed were so varied, it is difficult to classify him into just one category of a serial killer.

The short time frame between victims as well as the short length of his killing career is synonymous with a spree killer.

However, Knowles also possessed some classic traits of a serial killer such as a high IQ, normal social skills, and outward charm. Even though most would identify Knowles as a serial killer, his methods and lack of M.O make him difficult to define.

After Marjorie Howe, Knowles confession tapes said that he then murdered a hitchhiker named Alma. He said he raped and strangled her and left her body in the woods.

Police found no records of a missing woman with that name and it is believed that Knowles was lying to inflate his numbers, something many killers do especially those bent on achieving fame like Knowles.

However, police later found the body of ↗Blame
fourteen-year-old Ima Jean Sanders. Sanders frequently ran away from home in Warner Robins, Georgia, a town near the Georgia/Florida state line but always came back.

On August 1, 1974, Sanders was supposed to be babysitting her little sister while their parents were at work. Sanders had other ideas when her friends came to pick her up. Leaving her house that day would soon prove to be a fatal mistake.

It is believed that Knowles actually murdered Ima Sanders and that he mistook her name to be Alma. On his confession tapes, Knowles did refer to the hitchhiker he'd murdered as "Alma".

Luckily, her remains were found and confirmed. It is believed that Knowles did in fact murder more victims than he claimed and that there are many that have yet to be identified and/or discovered.

Several months later, Knowles returned to the crime scene to view Ima's body. He found that animals had eaten most of her remains but he was able to find her in-tact jaw bone which he took with him as a memento. — could have taken before

Taking trophies and mementos from victims is a very common trait in serial killers. Knowles did not take pieces of human bodies but rather objects that belong to the victims which he used such as the car that belonged to Alice Curtis.

Knowles taking a piece of one of his victim's remains was not in his normal M.O. In his confession tapes, he gave no reason why he did this.

In 1976, Ima Jean Sander's skeleton was found but she was not identified until 2011 when her mother and sister submitted DNA evidence to be matched against her remains. Police then matched Ima Jean's murder to that of Knowles's confessions tapes.

He did not kill his next victim until three weeks later. This longer amount of time between killings better fits the characteristics of a serial killer instead of that of a spree killer. Between killing Ima Jean Sanders and his next victim on August 23, he stayed with Jackie Knight and her children.

During these visits with Jackie, he would not tell her or her children much information about his life and his job.

Jackie later recalled that he made several jokes about being a robber. She didn't take these jokes too seriously because she knew there was most likely some truth to them.

Knowles staying with Jackie for several weeks could be another reason why he went back to where he murdered Ima Jean Sanders as Macon, Georgia were Jackie and her children lived is fairly close to where Ima was killed and buried.

After staying with her for three weeks, Jackie indicated that Knowles had outstayed his welcome. He was back on the road again and very soon back to killing. On August 23, 1974 he met a twenty-four-year-old mother named Katherine Pierce in Mosella, Georgia.

Knowles strangled Pierce in her home with a telephone chord in front of her three-year-old

→ Blame! Hero

son whom Knowles kept alive. Even though the young boy saw him murder his mother, Knowles spared his life. Throughout all of his murders, the only demographic Knowles did not murder were young, male children.

It is unknown why he avoided murdering young boys but it could have been tied back to his childhood aggression towards girls, they could have reminded him of his childhood friends, or reminded him of his painful, traumatic times in the reform school and felt that by sparing them he was getting some sort of vengeance on those who abused him as a child.

Knowles left Pierce's body in her bathroom, took her cash, and headed north. Two weeks later he ended up in Lima, Ohio. There, Knowles was seen with William Bates who disappeared on September 3, 1974, after leaving a bar with Knowles.

Witnesses recalled seeing the yellow Dodge Demon at the bar where Knowles and Bates met the night Bates went missing. The police found the car in the bar's parking lot the next day as Knowles left it there and took Bates's car, a red Chevrolet Impala.

The body of William Bates wasn't found until Thanksgiving Day 1974 when a hunter stumbled upon it in the woods.

Bates was found naked and having been strangled. It is believed that the men either had sex or were planning to before Knowles killed him. Those who knew him stated that Knowles would never admit to how he identified sexually as he'd had sexual relationships with men in prison. Bates wouldn't be the last of his victims that Knowles would supposedly have a sexual relationship with.

Knowles took with Bates's credit cards, car, and cash. He then continued his murderous cross-country trip and headed West for the first time. He traveled through Montana and Utah before ending up in Ely, Nevada.

While traveling West, Knowles would steal license plates of cars and screw them onto Bates's car in order to avoid suspicion and the police.

Once arriving in Ely, Nevada, Knowles discovered he was running low on cash and that the credit cards he had stolen from Bates were maxed now. The need for cash and the urge to kill both struck Knowles and he sought out to fulfill both of those needs.

On September 18, 1974, Knowles murdered a married couple in their sixties, Lois and Emmett Johnson. The Johnson's were from California and on a camping vacation in Nevada when Knowles tied both of them up, shot both behind the left ear and ran off with their cash.

Their bodies were not found until a week later. As with many of the murders committed by Knowles, police had no leads until his confession tapes were found. The same would happen with his next victim.

He then moved onto Texas where he met a woman named Charlynn Hicks on September 21 in the town of Seguin He is believed that Knowles killed Hicks after he found her on the side of the road after her motorcycle had stalled. Knowles raped and strangled Hicks and then drug her body through a barbed wire fence next to the road.

Her body was found four days later. No other information about the murder of Charlynn Hicks was recovered from the destroyed confession tapes.

In only two months, Knowles had traveled through half of the United States and had murdered 10 people. Little did Knowles know that he was halfway through the murder spree that would make him into a famous outlaw as well as only had two months to live.

On September 23, Knowles met Ann Dawson from Birmingham, Alabama. This was the first time Knowles had a travel companion. The two traveled together for almost two weeks until Knowles grew tired of her. He killed Dawson on September 29 and threw her body into the

50
48

Mississippi River. Her remains have never been found.

Knowles ended up next in Marlborough, Connecticut several weeks after killing Ann Dawson. There, he knocked on a random door of a house that he picked at random. The home belonged to a woman named Karen Wine who was not home at the time, however, her sixteen-year-old daughter, Dawn was.

Knowles forced his way into the Wine home. He then proceeded to rape and strangle Dawn with a nylon stocking. Karen arrived home before Knowles left. Knowles also raped and strangled Karen Wine. The Wine's other daughter found the bodies.

Knowles stole several albums from the Wine's home. He later gave the records to Jackie Knight as a gift. This is also where he stole the tape recorder which he would use to make his confessions.

On October 18, he'd traveled to Woodford, Virginia. There he broke into the home of fifty-three-year-old Doris Hosey. He told Hosey that all he wanted was a gun and that if she would give him one, he would leave.

Hosey said her husband had a rifle that she didn't want in the house anymore. She gave Knowles the rifle, which he turned on her. He loaded the gun, shot her, and laid the gun down next to her body.

This is one of the only times that Knowles killed for the sake of killing. There were no sexual aspects to this murder nor did he steal anything from the crime scene like he usually did.

It is believed that Knowles was continually adding to his body count in order to increase the fame and notoriety he believed he would one day achieve from being the outlaw he'd always wanted to be. There is no doubt that Knowles obtained some pleasure and gratification from killing Hosey as he had been able to control her whether or not she lived.

Knowles ended up back in Florida a few weeks after killing Hosey. By then, Knowles had made his way through most of the United States. His next intended victims were in Key West, Florida, which is the southernmost land mass in the United States.

He picked up two hitchhikers in Key West with the plan to kill both of them. Things did not go his way when he was pulled off by a local police officer for a minor traffic violation. At this point, police had no idea who Paul John Knowles was. They also did not know that he had been committing murders all over the country.

When Knowles was pulled over in Key West, he was still driving the car that had belonged to William Bates that had the stolen license plates. Not knowing who Knowles was, the police officer let him go with a warning.

Panicked, Knowles drove to Miami where he dropped the hitchhikers off. While in Miami, Knowles started to feel the pressure of what he'd done. Knowles went to the office of Sheldon Yavitz, the lawyer Angela Covic had hired to get him out of prison earlier that year.

Knowles approached Yavitz and said, "I have something to tell you. Brace yourself. I'm a mass murderer."

As his clients were mainly other murderers and drug dealers, Yavitz was not phased by this proclamation. Yavitz urged Knowles to confess. Naturally, Knowles refused and said that he wanted to go down in a "blaze of glory" like his heroes Bonnie and Clyde and John Dillinger.

Yavitz wrote a will for Knowles who also supplied Yavitz with his various confession tapes. After leaving Miami, Knowles headed back to Georgia where he would kill one of his last victims.

On November 6, 1974, Knowles met a man named Carswell Carr at a gay bar called The Pegasus in Milledgeville, Georgia. Car invited Knowles back to his house to spend the night.

Once Knowles arrived at Carr's home, he stabbed him twenty-seven times. Carr's body was later found naked. An autopsy showed that Carr actually died of a heart attack while being stabbed.

Unbeknownst to Knowles, Carr's fifteen-year-old daughter, Amanda was home. Knowles kicked down Amanda's bedroom door. He strangled her to death with stockings and then shoved the stockings so far down her throat that they had to be removed by a doctor.

Knowles then attempted to engage in necrophilia with Amanda's corpse. Police reports as well as the account of the confession tapes indicate that his attempts to perform necrophilia with Amanda's body were "unsuccessful" but provided no other information.

This is the first and last time Knowles attempted necrophilia on one of his victims. This sudden increase in sexual violence could be interpreted as Knowles having issues with his own sexuality, or that he wanted to punish and dominate someone to act out those urges and frustrations.

Knowles also was known to have had some sexual performance issues with women. His violent and degrading murder of Amanda Carr could have been Knowles violently acting out his sexual grievances with women.

Knowles also ransacked Car home. He stole Carwell's credit cards, car, cash, house keys, watch, shaving kit, briefcase, and most of his clothing. For several weeks, Knowles actually pretended to be Carswell Car by living in his house, using his credit cards, and driving his car.

Pretending to be a victim was also a new territory for Knowles. He then drove Carr's vehicle to Atlanta, Georgia. There Knowles met Sandy Fawkes, a woman whose life he would spare and a woman who would later write a book about him.

Fawkes was a British reported who had worked all over the world. She was in Atlanta looking for an assignment after leaving Washington, D.C after attempting to complete what she called "a botched assignment" for the National Inquirer.

Knowles and Fawkes met at a bar in an Atlanta Holiday Inn on November 8, 1974. Fawkes said that she was immediately attracted to him. She described him as looking like a combination of Robert Redford and Ryan O'Neal. She also that she was "immediately taken with this gaunt, good looks."

Knowles told her that his name was Daryl Golden and that he was a businessman from New Mexico who was in Atlanta to oversee a court case involving a restaurant chain his father owned. Knowles flirted heavily with Fawkes and invited her out to dinner.

At first, she rejected him and said, "you could be another Boston Strangler for all I know."

Little did she know, she had, in fact, stumbled upon a brutal killer who would one day be in the ranks of infamous serial killers along with the Boston Strangler.

Knowles persisted in pursuing Fawkes. She relented and that night she went to dinner with a serial killer. Later that evening, Knowles and Fawkes ended up in her hotel room. Fawkes recalled that she told him, "you're not a Boston Strangler after all, how disappointing."

Validity memory
F sensationalism

57

Fawkes was no doubt in for the surprise of her life when she found out who the man she'd spent the night with really was! Fawkes recalled in her book that Knowles suffered from bouts of impotence during their time together.

These reported incidents of impotence are most likely connected to issues related to his sexuality which Knowles experienced throughout his brief life.

Knowles himself never admitted whether or not he was heterosexual or homosexual but did admit to having sexual relationships with both men and women,

Knowles and Fawkes spent a week together traveling around. He was still driving William Bates's stolen car as well as using the identity and credit cards of Daryl Golden and Carswell Car.

It was suspected for some time that Daryl Golden was actually a victim of Knowles. The real Daryl Golden only had his wallet and identity stolen by Knowles and luckily not his life. No evidence has ever been found connecting anyone by the name of Daryl Golden to Paul John Knowles.

It is possible that Daryl Golden was a possible victim of Knowles who has yet to be identified.

Knowles also gifted Fawkes with a Mickey Mouse watch that had belonged to his victim Amanda Carr.

The couple drove to Miami where they went clubbing. She described his dancing as "so good people would gather around him on the dance floor to watch."

Fawkes later recalled several instances of odd behavior exhibited by the man she knew as Daryl Golden. She said that he repeatedly stated that he felt he was going to die young. She also recalled that she saw him cut an article out of a newspaper about the murders of Carswell and Amanda Carr, something he did on a regular basis.

She also said that Knowles asked her to write a book about him because he felt he would be dead within a year, which he was right about. Knowles also told her that his lawyer in Miami had tapes that would "make him famous one day."

Fawkes recalled that Knowles repeatedly mentioned his impending early death. She also said that he also had repeated "premonitions about his death."

Knowles was right about the tapes. Along with the book written by Sandy Fawkes, the confession tapes are some of the only pieces of evidence left of his murder spree.

Fawkes said that she started to grow suspicious of him but was never afraid of him. In her book, she wrote that she thought he might have been a mafia hitman or that he was running from someone or something. Knowles was, in fact, running from something…himself and the many, horrific murders he had committed.

She said that even though she grew weary of him, he came across as "sympathetic and easy to talk to." The two got along well and bonded over their troubled childhoods as Fawkes had spent several years in an orphanage and also had been abused as a child by authority figures.

Fawkes later said that she suspected that their shared bonding over their traumatic experiences as children was one of the reasons he didn't kill her. She also believed that he could have spared her life because she was a writer and had the capability to tell his story and make him famous which is what he truly wanted from life.

Overall, Fawkes had good memories of Knowles and it seemed as if he did have some affection for her.

good guy

She wrote about him giving her his jacket when she was cold, helping her and showing sympathy towards her when she burned her finger, and described how he saved the life of a moth.

Fawkes wrote that Knowles was "too gentle and too kind for violence." She soon changed

62

her mind when his true self-emerged behind is an artfully crafted facade.

Fawkes also wrote that when she figured out what Knowles was, she wrote that she had "been playing sulky games with a man whose rage could wreck a room."

After spending six days together, Fawkes decided that their short fling had fizzled out. Knowles didn't want to end their relationship. When he continued perusing Fawkes, she avoided him.

Sandy Fawkes was somewhat of a controversial figure herself. Fawkes grew up in orphanages and other public houses in 1940's England after she was found as a baby in the Grand Union Canal shortly after she was born on June 30, 1929.

Fawkes was a heavy drinker and known to frequent many pubs in London. The fact that Fawkes was an alcoholic had led many to discredit some of her journalistic endeavors and reports as well as he accounts of the six days she spent with Knowles.

Witnesses later reported her having been with Knowles in both Atlanta, Georgia and later un both West Palm Beach, Florida and Miami, Florida.

The book Fawkes wrote about her time spent with Knowles, called Killing Time has been met with mixed reviews since it was first published in 1979. The book has since been reprinted several times.

Sandy Fawkes died on December 26, 2005. She was 75 years-old.

During their short romance, Fawkes had introduced Knowles to two of her friends, James and Susan McKenzie.

The McKenzie's had grown to like Knowles and felt bad that Fawkes had broken off their relationship. The couple kept visiting with Knowles.

On November 15, Knowles gave Susan McKenzie a ride to her hairdressers. On the way, Knowles pulled a gun on her and demanded she have sex with him. McKenzie was able to free herself. She flagged down another couple in a car who was passing by.

McKenzie then went to the police. An A.B.P (All Points Bullet) was issued for the red Impala. She was also able to give police his real name.

Knowles was pulled over later that day. When the officer approached his car, he pulled a sawed-off shotgun on the officer despite being on a busy street in the middle of the car.

He drove away with the police chasing and following him. Knowles then drove into a random carport, left the stolen car behind and fled on foot.

That same day, November 15, Knowles forced his way into the home of a woman named Beverly Mabee in West Palm Beach, Florida. He told Mabee he had just committed a robbery and needed a place to hide out.

Knowles tied Mabee up even though she was in a wheelchair. He psychically assaulted her and waited for Mabee's sister, Barbara Tucker who Mabee said was coming by to see her later that night.

When Tucker arrived, Knowles greeted her with his shotgun. Tucker had her six-year-old son with her so she begged him not to kill her and to take her money, credit cards, and car instead.

Knowles tied up the young boy along with his aunt and kidnaped Tucker. Towards the end of killing spree, Knowles actually left several people alive which is interesting considering he showed hardly no discrimination ion in murdering his earlier victims.

After Knowles left with Barbara Tucker in her car, her son was able to wiggle out of the ropes he was bound in. He went to the neighbor's house where they called the police.

While Knowles and Tucker were in the car together, he kept flipping through radio stations to see if there were any reports about him and

67

the crime he'd just committed. Tucker said that she just kept talking to Knowles about anything and everything to distract him from killing her.

Tucker said that he kept the conversation going as well. When he asked her what she did for a living and she told him that she was a copywriter, she recalled that he grew excited and asked her to write a book about him.

Knowles and Tucker traveled through the night together and ended up in Fort Pierce, Florida. The next day, Knowles set Barbara Tucker free without harming her. Like Susan Fawkes, Tucker believed that Knowles did not kill her because she was a writer.

While Tucker and Knowles were in her car, the police found the red Chevrolet Impala. In the car, police found a copy of the will Sheldon Yavitz had made for him.

After over four months, a trial of bodies, and over half the fifty states, police finally had the name of the man who had been alluding them for so long.

Apprehension and Death

Once Knowles was identified, the FBI ran his name through the national database and found his previous criminal convictions. The FBI then put out a nationwide search for Knowles. Beverly Mabee was able to identify Knowles from the photo from his prison files.

Police in Lima, Ohio contacted the FBI about the yellow Dodge Demon found near the body of William Gates. Fingerprints were collected from the car and matched to William Gates' car as well as Barbara Tucker's.

Also found in the Gates car were several press clippings about the Carr murders. Police questioned Sandy Fawkes who they briefly thought was an accomplice as Knowles had kept her alive.

At this point, Fawkes was unaware of Knowles true identity. She still knew him as Daryl Golden. Police showed her several photos of the Carr crime scene as well as photos of the Carr family and she identified some of the clothes that Carswell Carr was wearing as having belonged to Knowles.

Shortly after the fingerprints on the cars were matched, a store clerk called the police with a tip that a redheaded man had been in the store where he was working and has used Carswell Carr's credit card to buy cassette tapes.

Police also tracked down Jackie Knight. She was able to give them a rough estimate timeline of where Knowles was during certain times. She told police that he had mentioned being at the home of Carswell Carr but didn't say that he murdered them.

The police were able to track the various credit card charges that Knowles had spent all across the country. By this point, police concluded that in only four months Knowles had travel through thirty-seven states and murdered ten people.

At the time, police didn't have much information about Knowles or where he might be. On November 16, just a day after Knowles attacked Beverly Mabee and kidnapped Barbara Tucker, the police were finally able to start searching for their killer.

Barbara Tucker and Knowles had spent the night together in a motel in Fort Pierce, Florida. Tucker later recalled how Knowles kept flipping between television channels to see if there were any reports about him on the news just like he'd done in the car the day before.

Tucker said that she even saw her own missing person's report on the news and grew even more scared. Luckily, Knowles released her without harming her. Tucker ran to local police who were astonished she was still alive.

Her testimony as well as that of her sister, Sandy Fawkes, and Susan McKenzie were able to apprehend a horrific and violent killer.

Several hours after Barbara Tucker was released, police pulled over Knowles who was driving Tucker's red Volkswagen. Knowles had made it to Perry, Florida, a town located forty-five minutes away from the Georgia border.

When Knowles was pulled over by Florida Highway Patrol Trooper Charles Eugene Campbell, Knowles pulled out his sawed off shotgun and aimed it at Campbell. Knowles was then able to wrestle Campbell's gun away from him.

Going back one of the first crimes he ever committed, Knowles kidnapped and took the officer hostage at gunpoint. He handcuffed Campbell to the backseat of the car. Knowles drove off with Campbell in the back of his patrol car. While on the road, Knowles pulled over a man named James Meyers, an environmental engineer who was in Florida on a business trip.

Knowles also took Meyer hostage as well as took his car which he wanted because it was less suspicious than driving around with a kidnapped police officer in the back of a stolen police car.

Knowles actually had to stop for gas while he was driving the stolen police car. The cashier at the gas station noticed that the police officer was sitting in the backseat of the car but didn't say anything because the men in the car didn't.

When the cashier heard the report about the two hostages in the car, he called the police and reported what he'd seen.

He now had two hostages on his hands instead of just one who just so happened to be a cop. Knowles knew what he had to do to eliminate the witnesses. He took Meyer and Campbell out into the woods in a remote area of Pulaski County, Georgia.

He then handcuffed both men to a tree and shot both of them in the head at close range.

After killing the police officer and the innocent bystander, Knowles hopped into Meyers's stolen car and continued driving on.

Several hours after killing Campbell and Meyer, Knowles reached a police roadblock in Henry County, Georgia.

Not knowing where he would go, multiple law enforcement agencies set up roach blocks in several counties in an attempt to catch Knowles.

He attempted to drive through the barricades but lost control of the vehicle and crashed into a tree.

Knowles escaped the crash on foot. He was chased by law enforcement officers from several agencies as well as police dogs and helicopters. While escaping Knowles fired multiple shots at the perusing officers with Campbell's pistol he had stolen.

A Georgia State Trooper actually shot Knowles in the leg. The bullet grazed him and Knowles kept going.

Then Knowles stumbled into a boarded-up farmhouse. There he realized that Campbell's gun was out of bullets. He found a shotgun and a box of shells in the farmhouse. He then went to a nearby house to ask for help.

At that house, he met David Clark. A Vietnam veteran who'd just returned from a hunting trip and had a gun handy. Knowles first asked Clark for help and then tried to shoot him.

The gun became jammed and Clark pulled his own weapon on Knowles. Clark led him to his neighbor's house at gunpoint where she called the police.

It was later revealed that Knowles was actually several miles outside of the perimeter of the search and that if it wasn't for the armed civilian catching Knowles, he might not have ever been caught.

It is also possible that if David Clark hadn't by chance run into Knowles, he might have never been apprehended and would have escaped again.

He was arrested and kept in the Henry County, Georgia jail. When he arrived there were tons of reporters there who bombarded him with questions like a celebrity. Knowles was clearly reveling in the attention and ended up getting exactly what he wanted…to be a famous outlaw.

The press and media dove headfirst into the case and immodestly started to sensationalize the handsome man who's taken cops hostage, stolen countless objects, and murdered over a dozen people. It was then that Knowles earned the nickname the Casanova Killer. Knowles most likely loved having finally been caught as he finally was able to get the attention he thought he deserved.

Once he was apprehended, Knowles refused to reveal several key pieces of information to police about the crimes that he'd committed and where he'd buried and dumped some of the bodies of his victims. This allowed him to have some sort of control, which he loved having just as much as attention.

While being interrogated, Knowles refused to give too much information to authorities. This went on for several weeks. He told police about the tapes which he said "contained his legacy."

The police contacted Sheldon Yavitz in Miami who refused to hand over the tapes as it was stated in Knowles will that the tapes would only be released after Knowles died. Yavitz was asked several times to hand over the tapes and refused. This led to him being arrested for contempt of court and tampering with evidence.

Once arrested, Yavitz still wouldn't budge. Police then arrested his wife for contempt of court. After his wive's arrest, Yavitz broke down and said he'd go against his client's wishes and released the tapes as long as his wife was released.

The bribe worked but Yavtiz couldn't afford his bond payment so he stayed in jail for several weeks. Knowles was transferred to several different prisons as a way to avoid too much attention. He also had to travel to several locations to obtain charges for the various murders he'd committed.

While Knowles refused to reveal several key pieces of information about his crimes to police, he absolutely refused to provide the location of the body of Trooper Campbell as well as the location of the handgun he'd stolen from Campbell and dropped in the woods during his foot pursuit.

Knowles eventually gave in and agreed to help police locate the body of Trooper Campbell as well as the location of his gun which Knowles had stolen.

After Knowles was arrested, he reportedly enjoyed the attention and notoriety that his crimes brought him. Like other highly sensationalized murders, this case brought tons of attention which was exactly what Knowles wanted.

While in jail, hundreds of people lined the streets hoping to get a look at the newly minted Casanova Killer. These crowds grew once word spread among women how handsome the Casanova Killer was.

In the book Manhunters: Criminal Profilers and Their Search for the World s Most Wanted Serial Killers by Colin Wilson describes there being "crowds of local coeds four feet deep" that were lined up outside of the jail and courthouse hoping to catch a glimpse of the handsome killer.

Although Knowles murdered people of all ages and sexes, the media took the stories of the multiple women in his life, and in classic media, fashion sensationalized his relationships with them.

These stories combined with his good looks, which were described by Sandy Fawkes as being "a combination of Robert Redford and Ryan O'Neal" cemented his nickname.

Naturally, since Knowles loved and reveled in the attention he'd wanted for his crimes for so long, he did not shy away from talking to the press and giving interviews. He told one reporter that he was "the only successful member of his family."

He also said that his goal in having committed his crimes was "to become known, to get myself a name."

In a remark similar to him predicting (albeit predicting it correctly) that he would die young and soon, Knowles also told a reporter that he wouldn't live to go to trial for his crimes. Again, he was right.

On December 18, 1974, Knowles finally got the famous outlaw exit he probably loved.

That day, Sheriff Earl Lee and Georgia Bureau of Investigation Agent Ronnie Angel were traveling on Interstate 20 in Georgia. They were in a police cruiser but the car did not have a cage in the back. While in the cruiser, Sheriff Lee noticed that somehow Knowles had lit a cigarette even though he was handcuffed.

Lee asked Knowles to hand over the cigarette. He did, he moved forward. One of his wrists were free as he'd picked the lock on his cuffs with a paper clip when the officers weren't paying attention. Knowles grabbed Sheriff Lee's handgun and fired it twice while it was still in the holster.

Lee lost control of the vehicle and ran off the road. Agent Angel grabbed his gun and shot Knowles three times including once in the head. It is believed that he died instantly. He was only twenty-eight years-old.

Close

Agent Angel and Sheriff Lee were not charged for the shooting death of Paul John Knowles. His death and life were exactly what he wanted, that of a famous outlaw. Even though he never gained the fame or true crime cult status of his heroes Bonnie and Clyde, Jesse James, and John Dillinger, Knowles got exactly what he wanted.

After his death, Sheldon Yavtiz tried to sue the state of Georgia for killing Knowles before he could stand trial. The attempt was unsuccessful.

Yavitz was later sentenced to ten years in prison for tax evasion and money laundering after his shady dealings with even shadier clients came to light when several of his cases received national attention.

Many of Yavitz's former drug dealer and dealer connected clients testified against him in exchange for deals with the DEA (Drug Enforcement Administration).

The confession tapes were reviewed by a judge and other law enforcement officials and found that most of what Knowles claimed on them was true and that evidence added up to what Knowles claimed he did.

Before his death, Knowles claimed that he killed thirty-five people but police were only ever able to prove twenty out of thirty-five. Some records list a total of eighteen victims instead of twenty.

Due to the various locations where Knowles committed his murders and the ever-increasing numbers of unsolved murders and reported missing people, it is possible that Knowles was in fact actually responsible for thirty-five murders like he claimed.

It is very much possible that Knowles could have killed thirty-five and that they have yet to be found. Shortly after his death, officials in both Georgia and Alabama linked Knowles to the deaths of several hitchhikers who very well could have been some of his victims.

His constant need and drive for attention are one of the aspects of his personality and crimes that make Knowles stand out among similar criminals.

While the concept of wanting to get caught is common among both serial and spree killers alike, it seems as if Knowles took this to the next level and almost demanded it.

This brings up the thought that if Knowles had another outlet for his aggressions, a proper mental health diagnosis and treatment, and a stable life from the beginning, the Casanova Killer might have never been or might not have murdered 18 to 35 people.

Since his desire for attention was so strong, it could have been the primary reason behind his murder spree and his early crimes of kidnapping and burglary.

This in itself would seemingly put Knowles in a category all his own when it comes to serial killers.

The motive for most killers can be easily defined, such as Jeffrey Dahmer killing for control and power over another human being, Ted Bundy killing for the thrill or a killer for profit such as a black widow killer.

When to comes to the motives behind the killings for Knowles, there really wasn't one. Based on some of his later murders where he raped, sexually assaulted and one time attempted necrophilia it seemed as if Knowles was, in fact, escalating his crimes and that the motive had become about the thrill of the kill and possibly motivated by both sex and lust.

Based on what Knowles himself said it appears that he did kill purely for attention and to achieve his lifelong goal of eventually becoming a famous outlaw like the ones he idolized growing up.

As time went on and Knowles continued killing, that motive evolved. The more he killed the more he liked it and his motive and M.O changed from killing for fame and attention to killing for the thrill, lust, power, and control.

Although based on Knowles's early life, his upbringing, and the abuse he experienced while at the Florida School for Boys his life seemed predestined to go into the direction of growing up to be a violent criminal.

Like with every other serial, mass, and spree killer Knowles's upbringing also brings up the question of nature versus nurture along with the endless questions of "what if?"

All in all, Paul John Knowles lived a brief, yet morbidly curious life. Had he lived longer, Knowles might have either never been caught. Or if he had been caught, we might have more information into the mind of such a deranged and truly undefinable killer.

The fact that there is a limited amount of information about Knowles available in comparison to other serial killers, makes him and his story all the more fascinating.

Not knowing all the grisly details about his crimes and having a vast majority of the information about Knowles and his crimes come second hand, makes him even more terrifying as your imagination is left to wonder and fill in the blanks.

Printed in Great Britain
by Amazon

87122198R00058